Color Like an Artist

Coloring Book for Adults

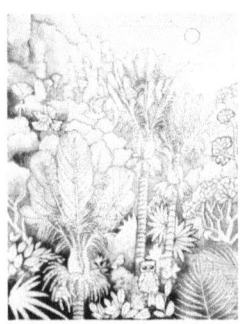

Irina Velman

Published by Creative Soul Publishing Inc. in 2015
First Edition; First Printing

Illustrations and design ©2015 Irina Velman

www.creativesoulpublishing.com

ISBN 978-0473341138

Introduction

If you always wanted to learn drawing and painting, this coloring book is the perfect place to start.

Illustrations in this book are based on original paintings by New Zealand artist Irina Velman. The book contains traditional linear drawings as well as greyscale images with tonal values and shading for creating more realistic effect. Some of the paintings used for the designs are displayed on the back cover of the book, just for the general color guidance. Feel free to play and experiment with colors creating your own amazing art work. Beautiful landscapes, birds, flowers- these nature themes and patterns will give you hours of relaxation and creative coloring. Have fun!

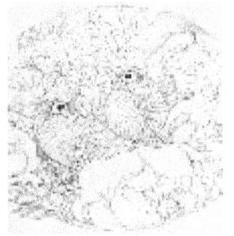

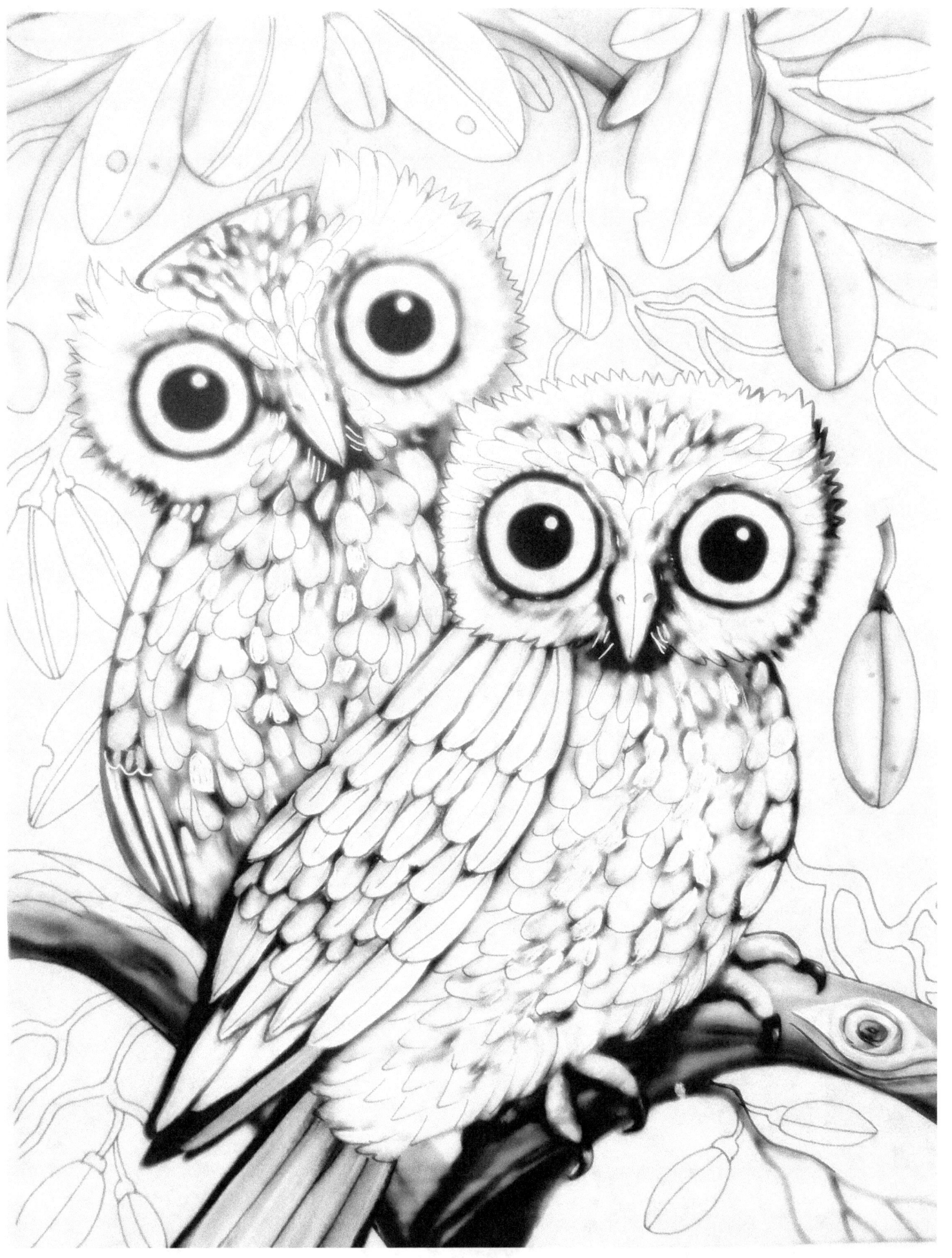

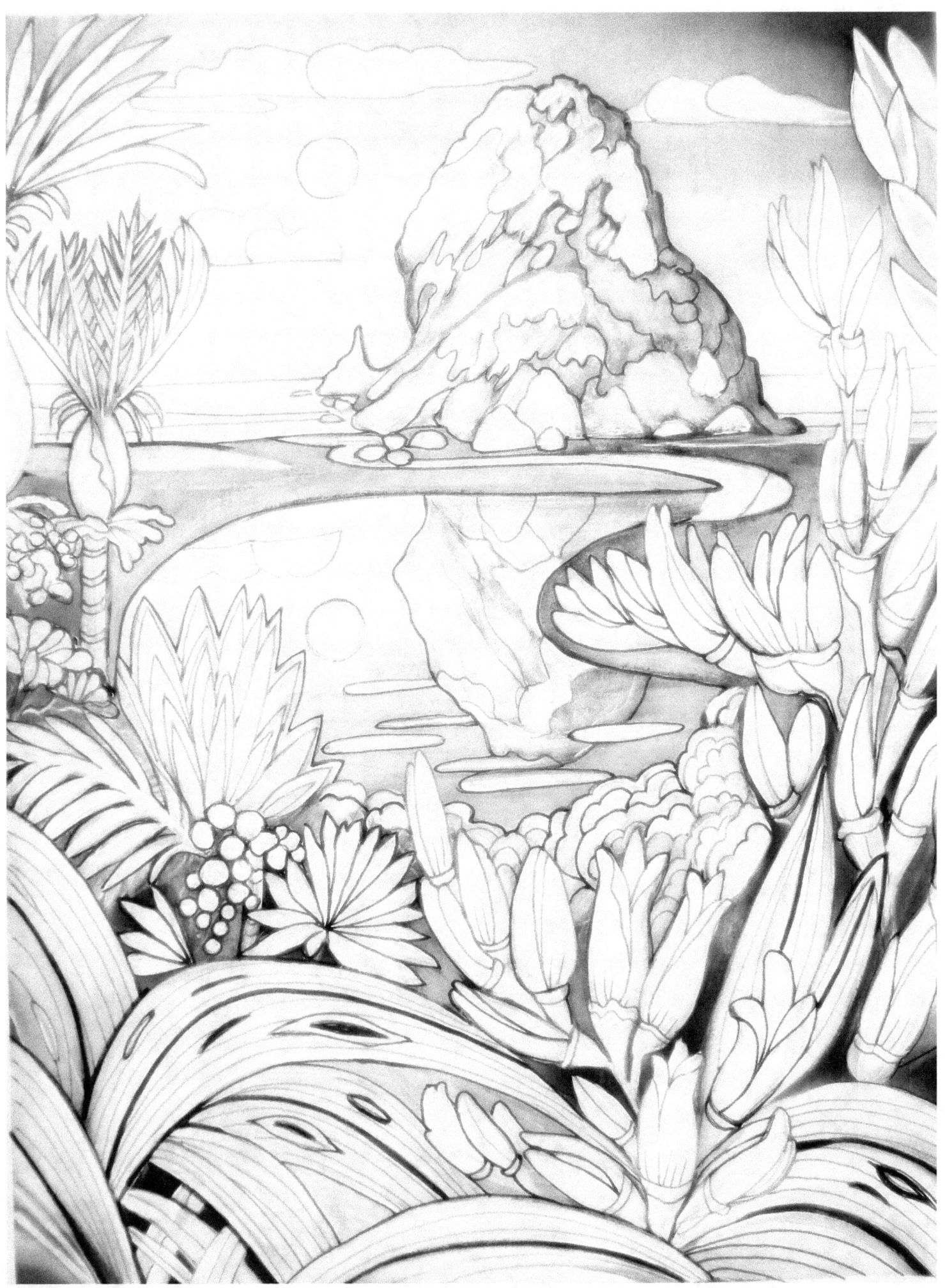

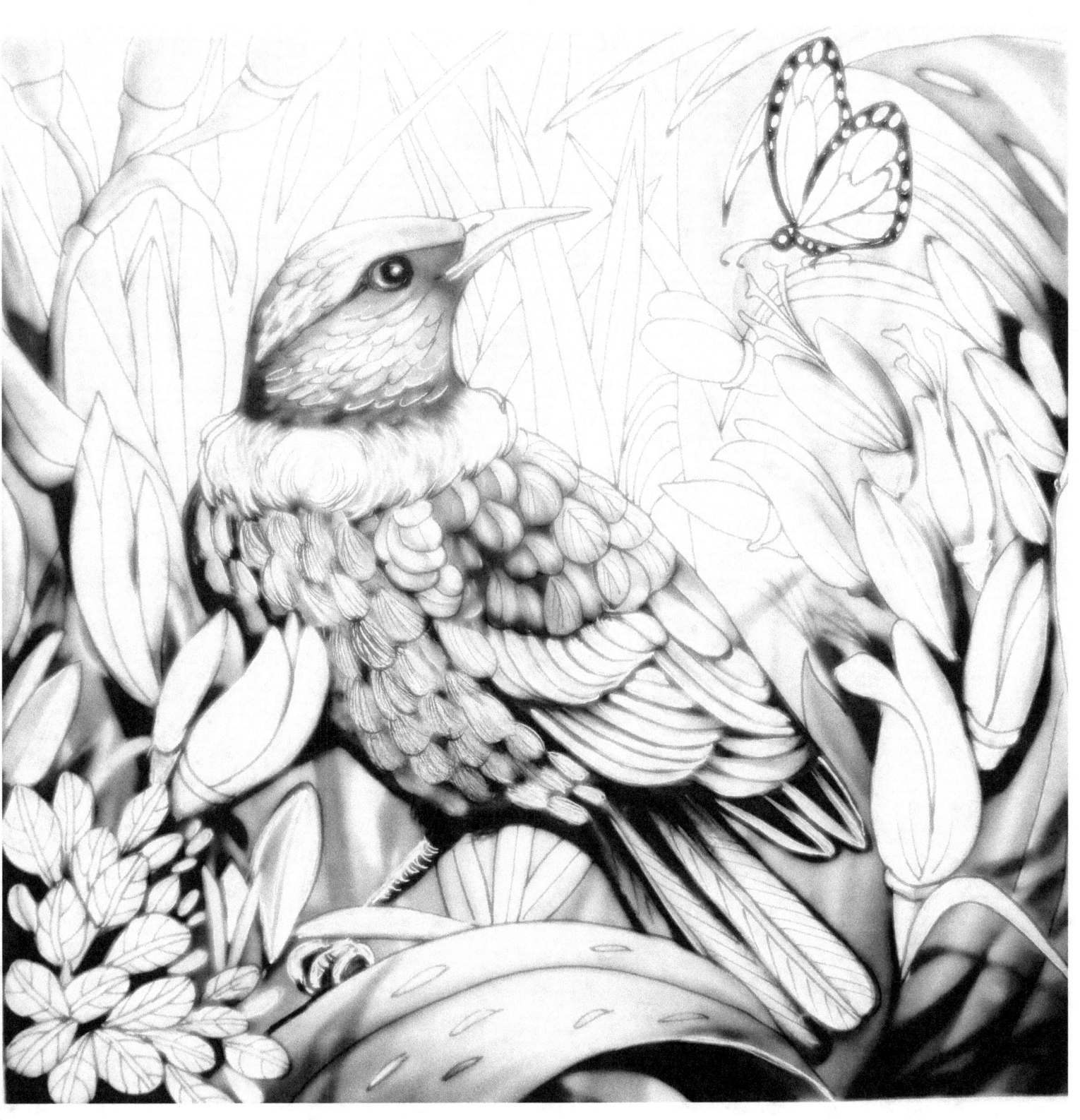

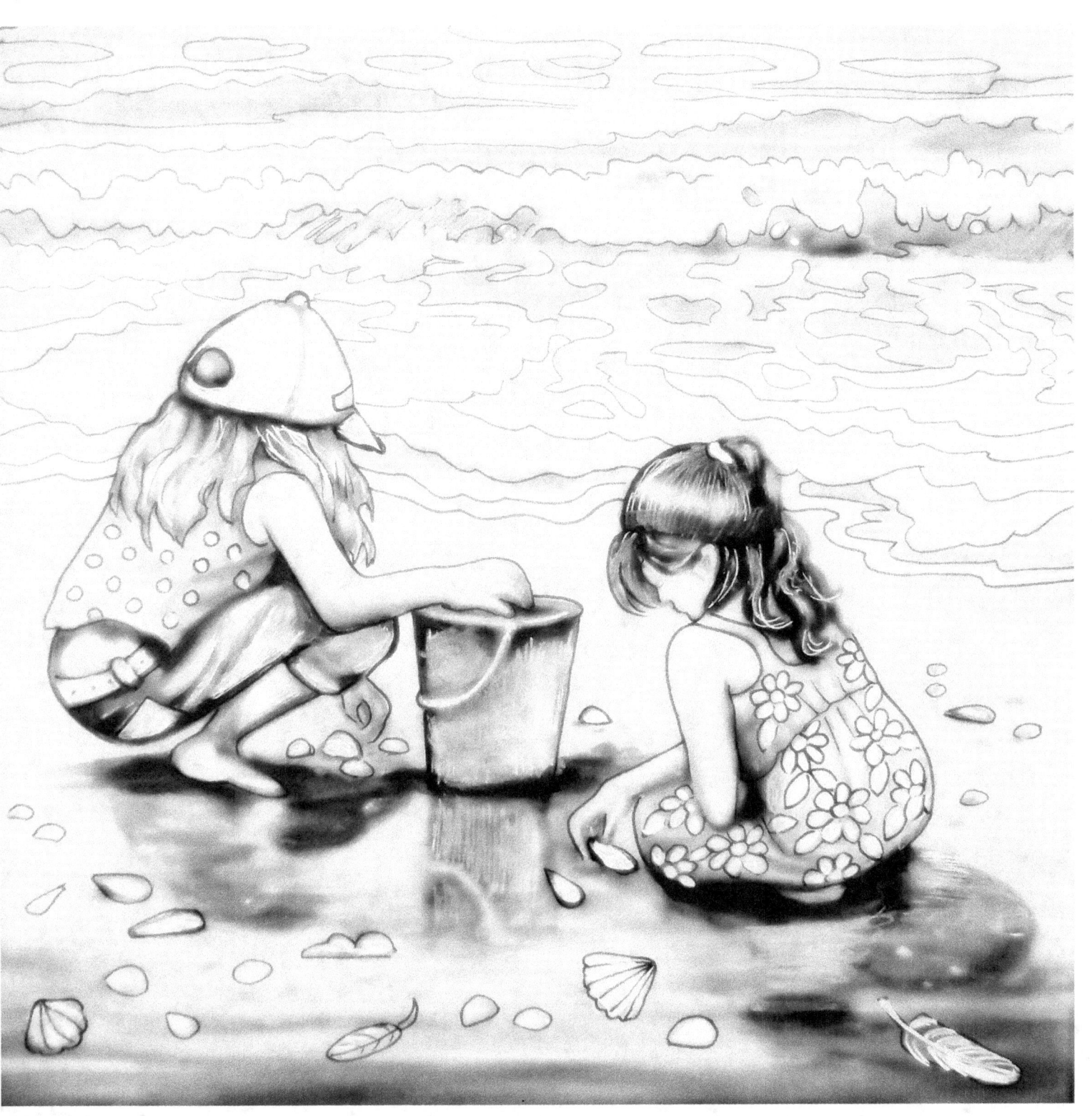

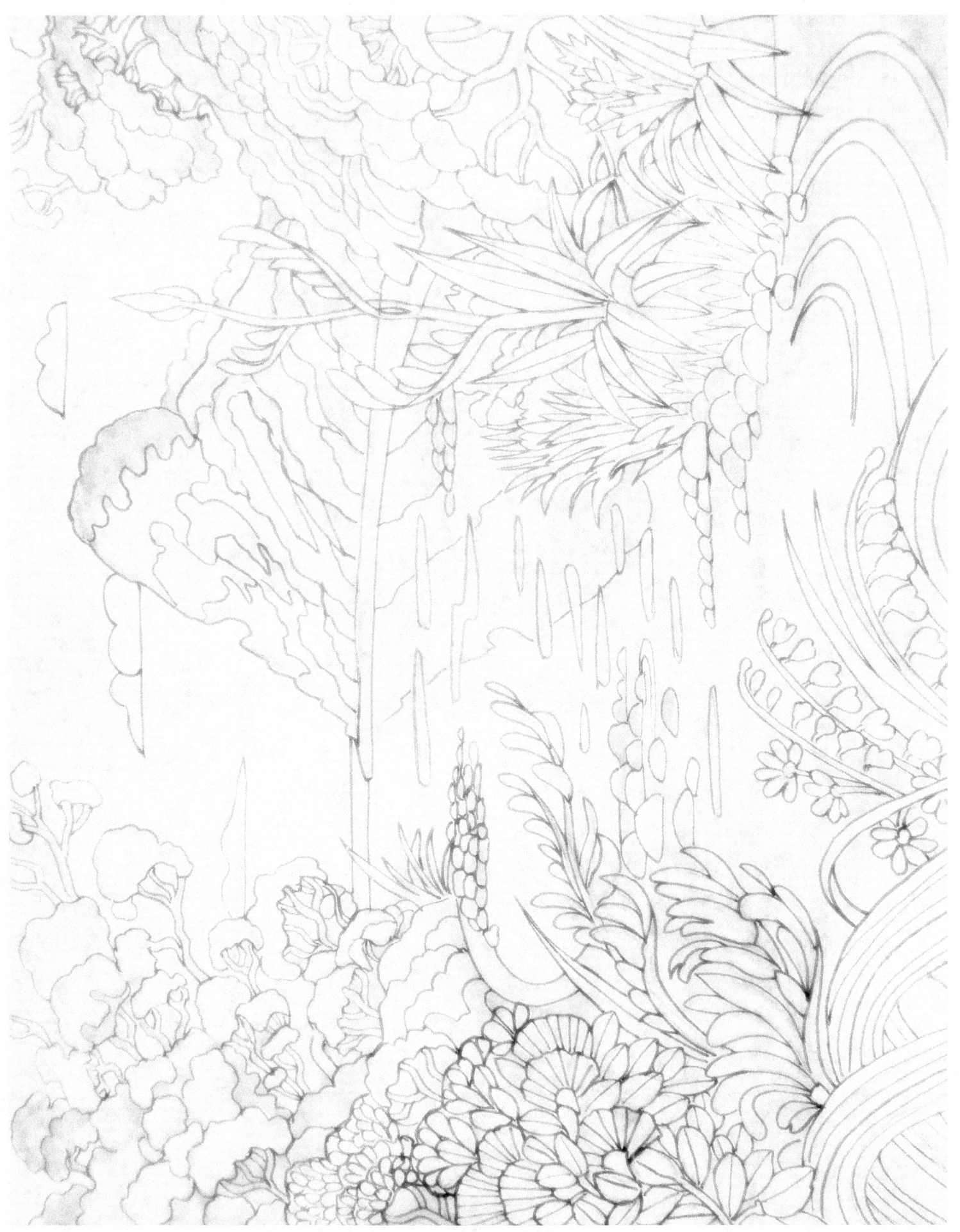

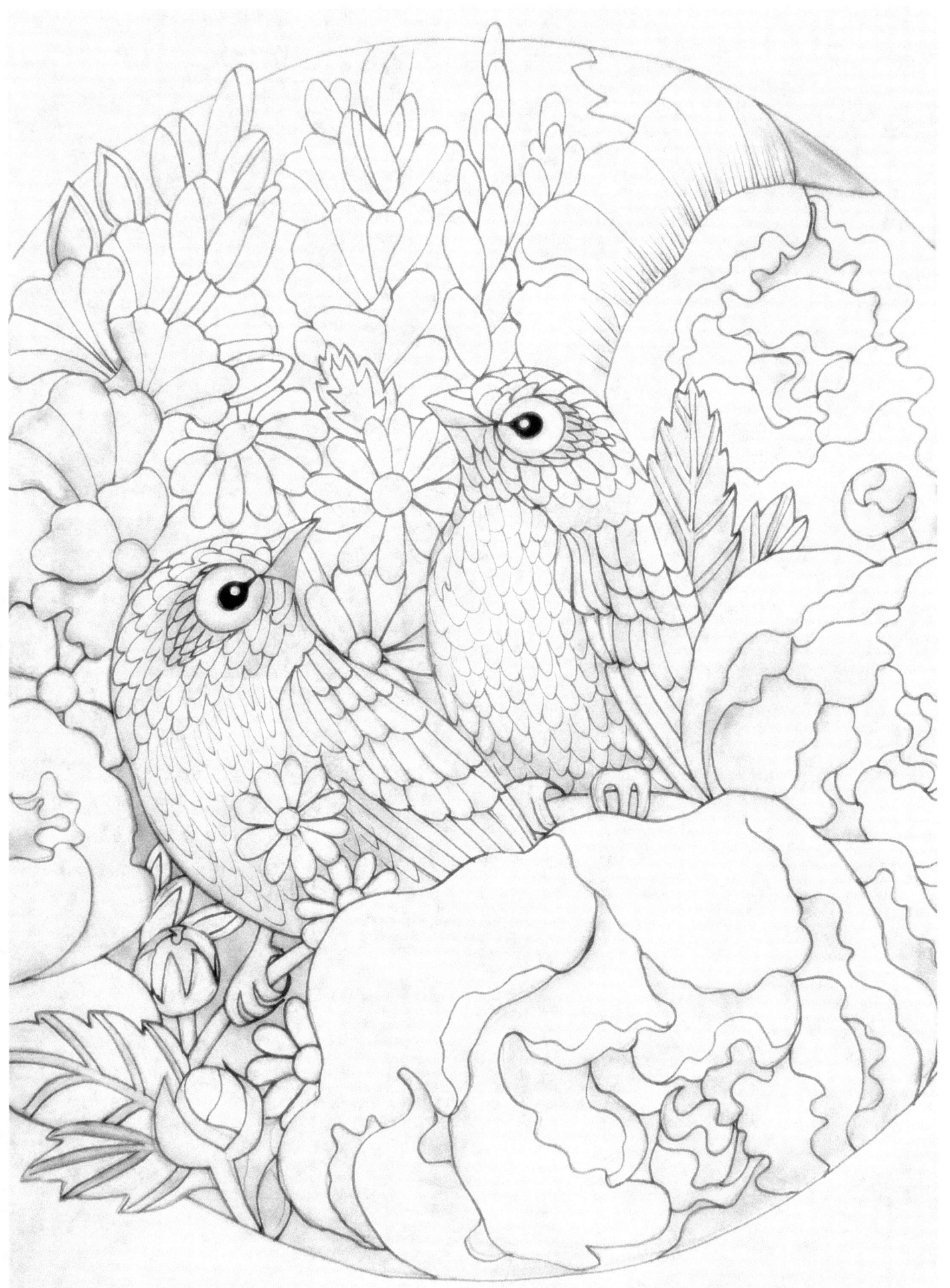

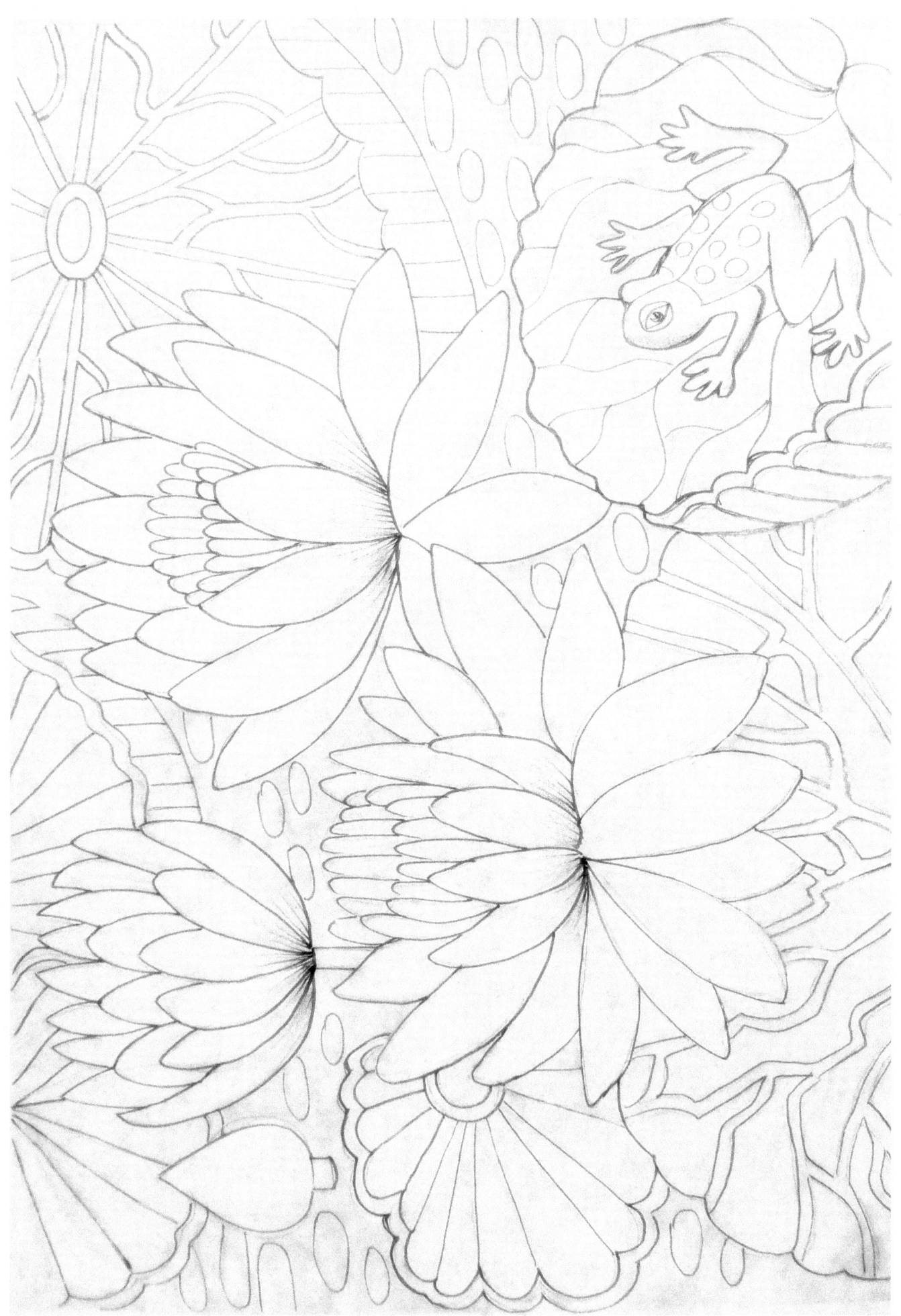

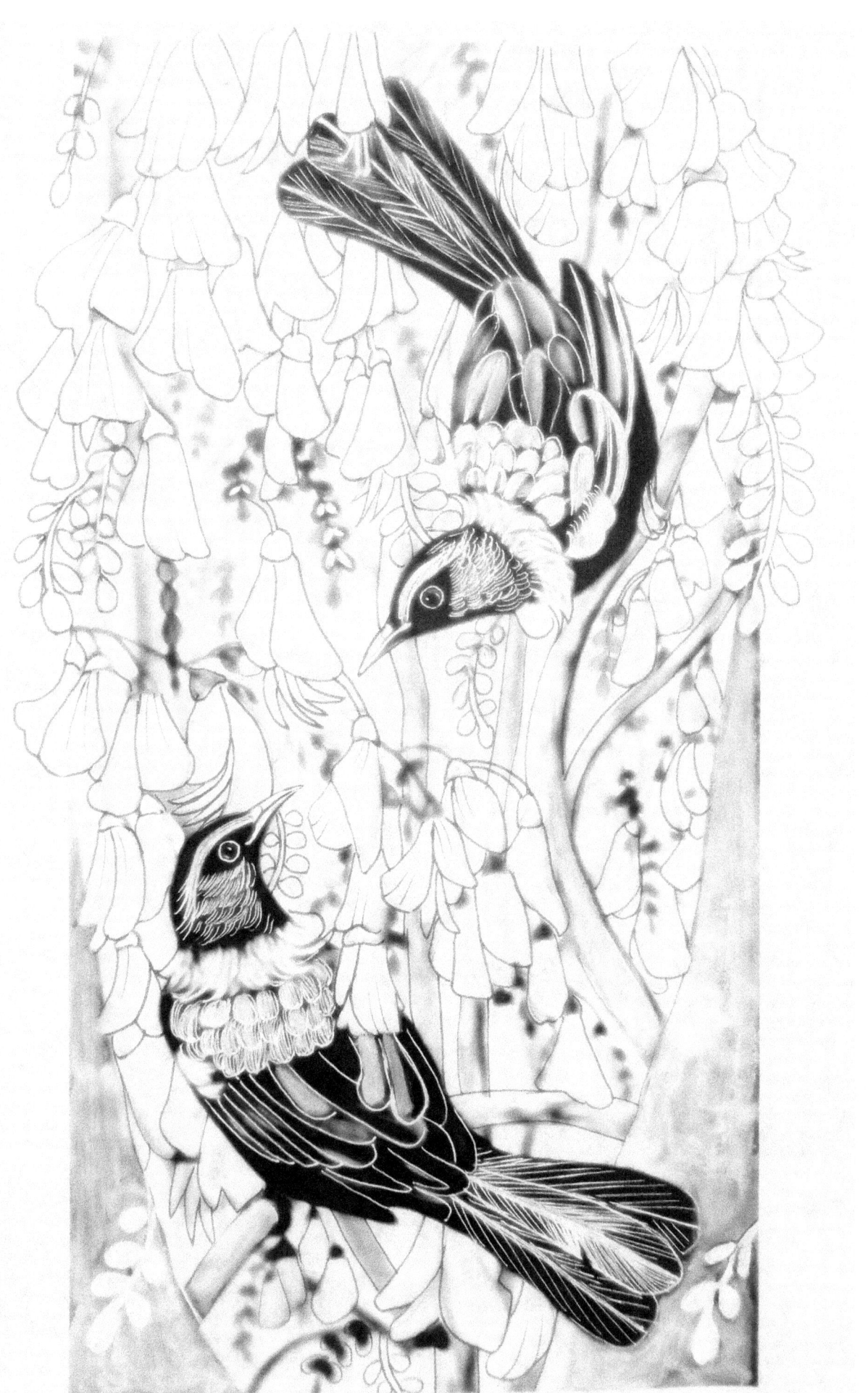

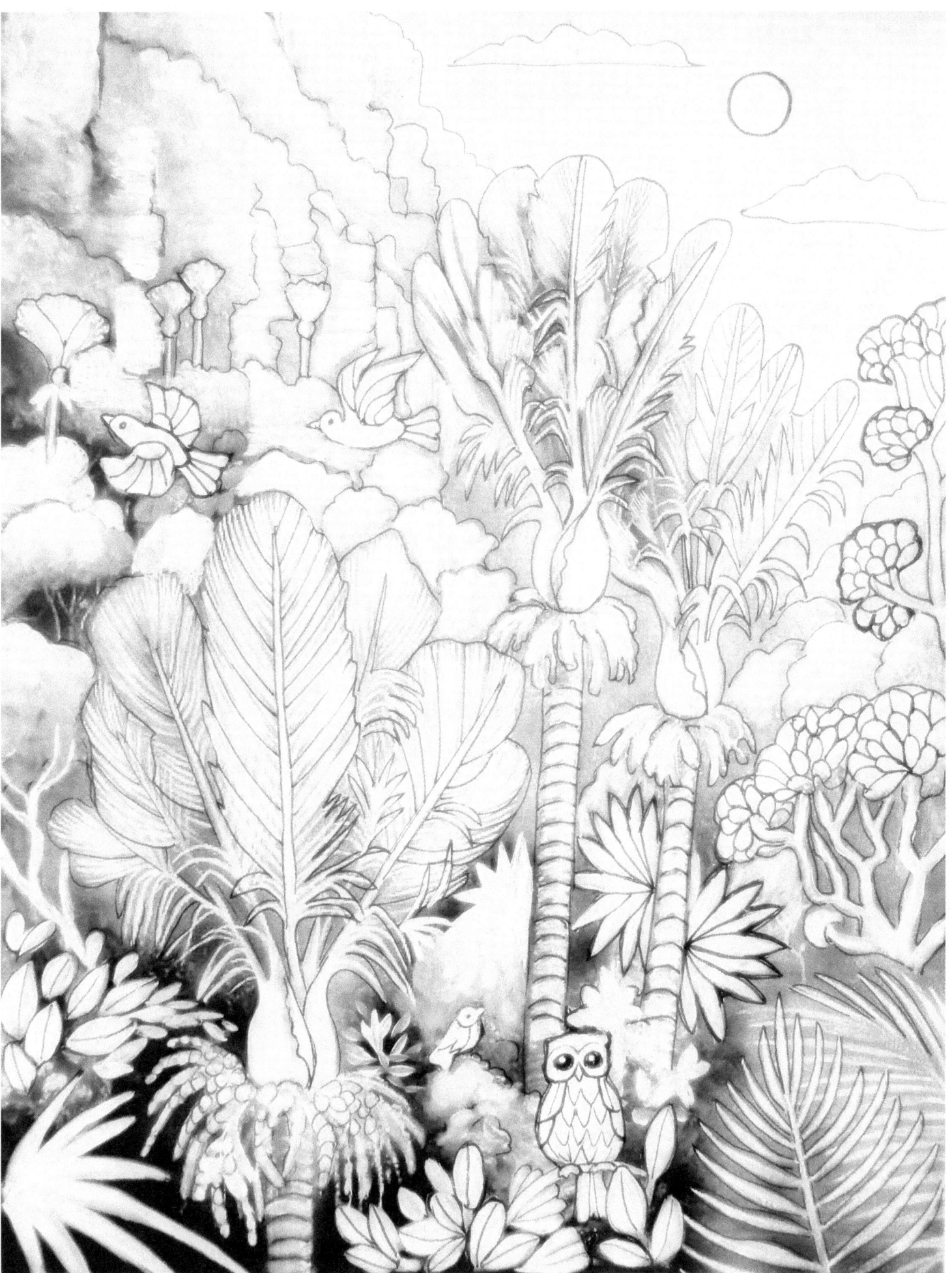

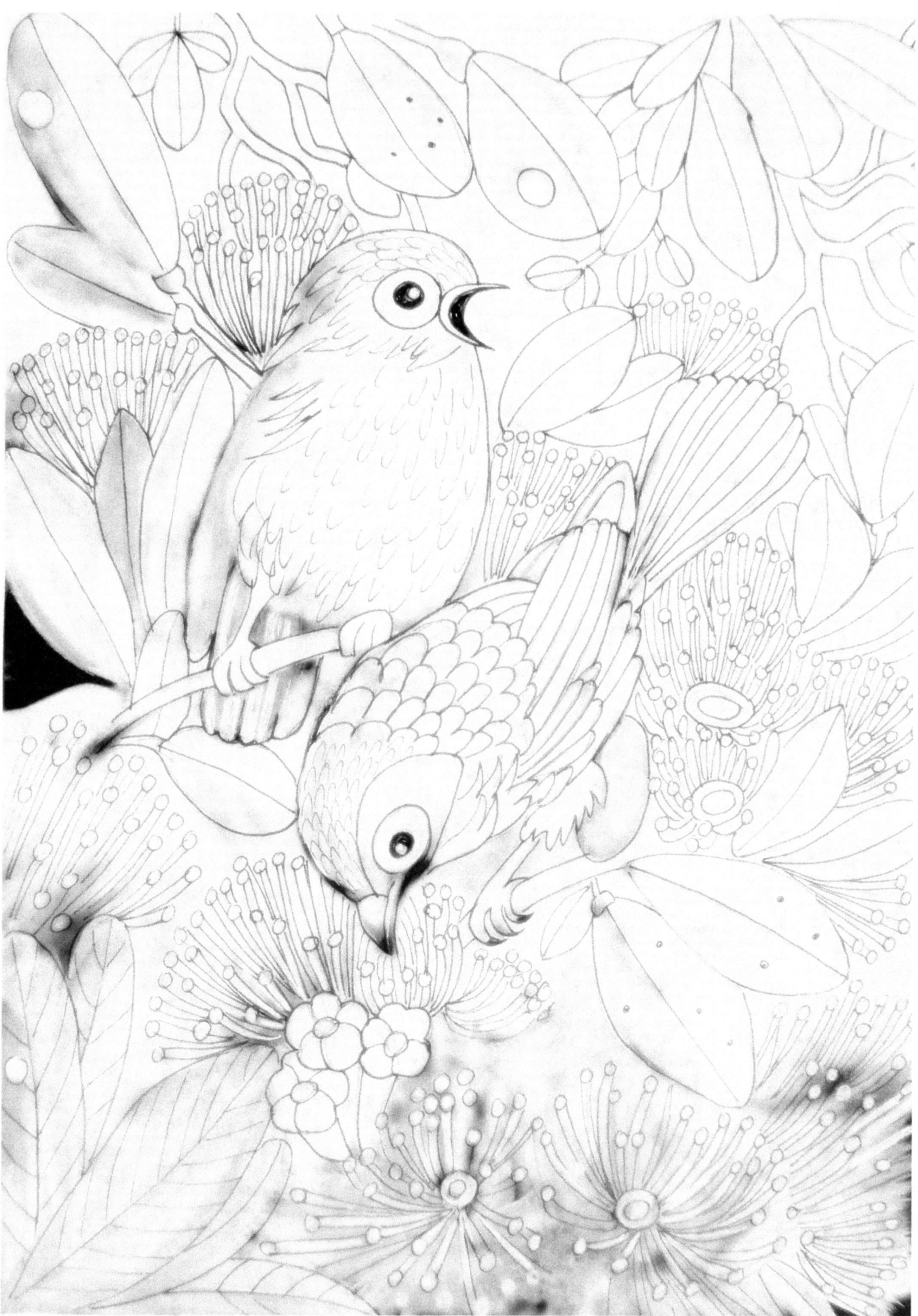

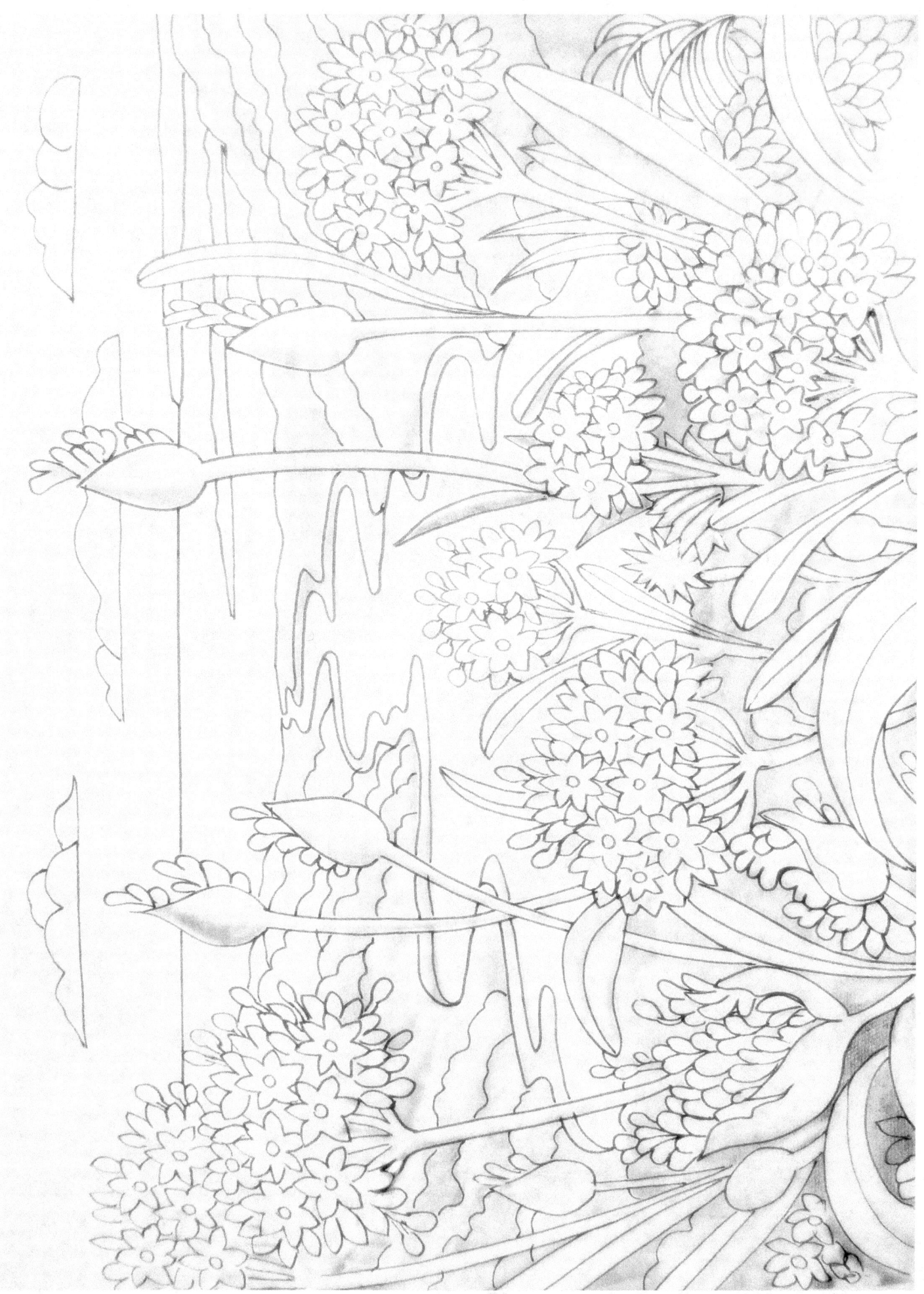

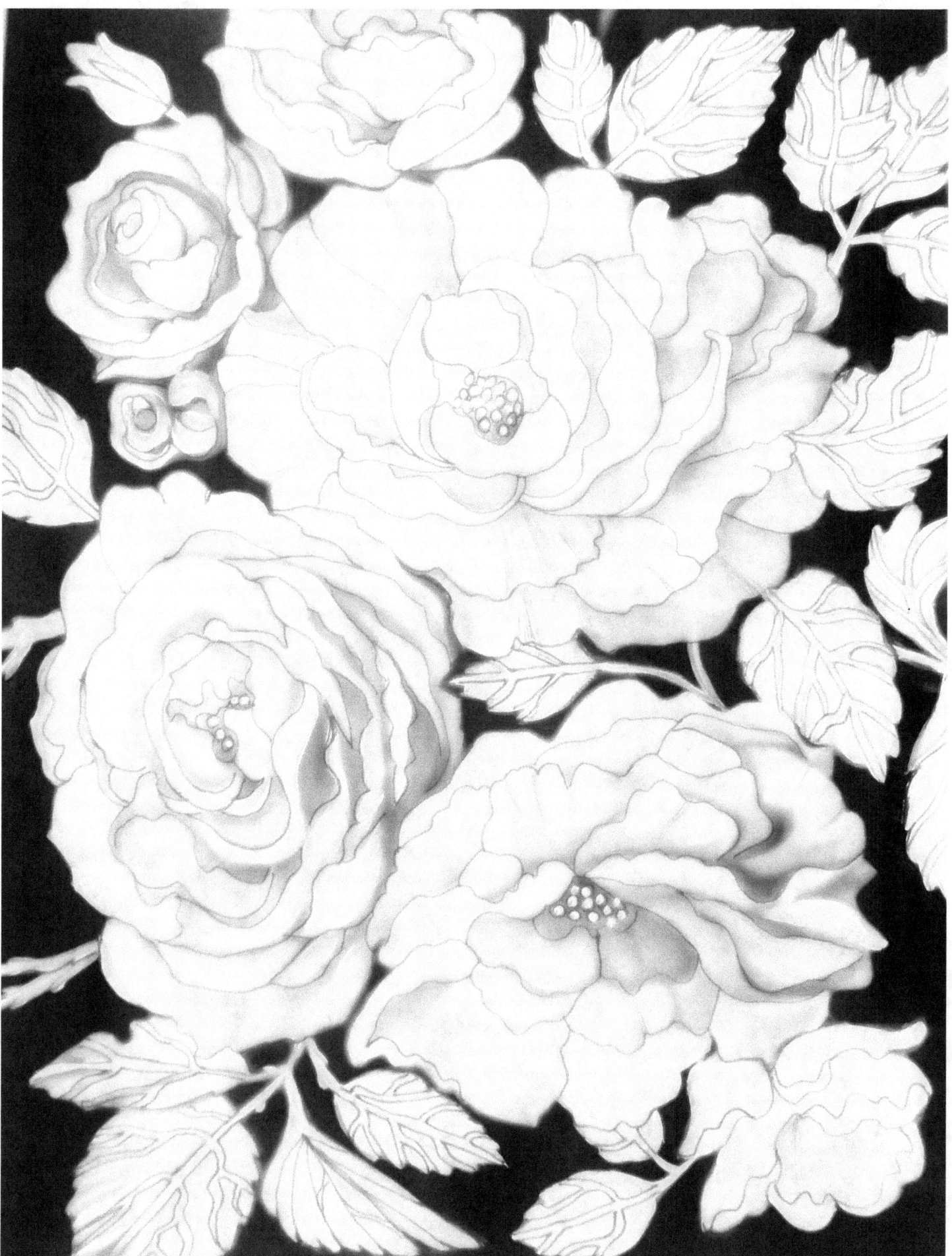

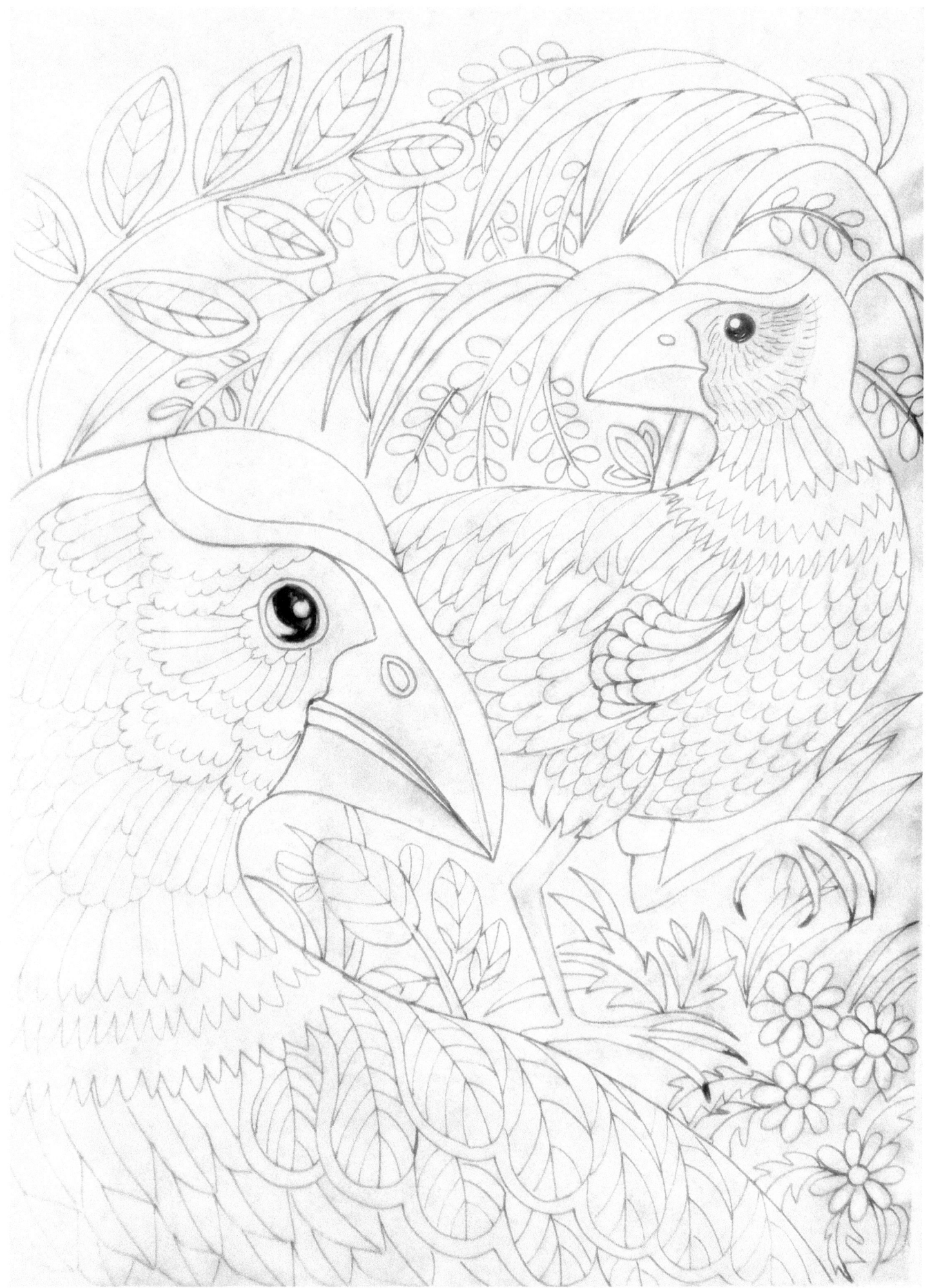

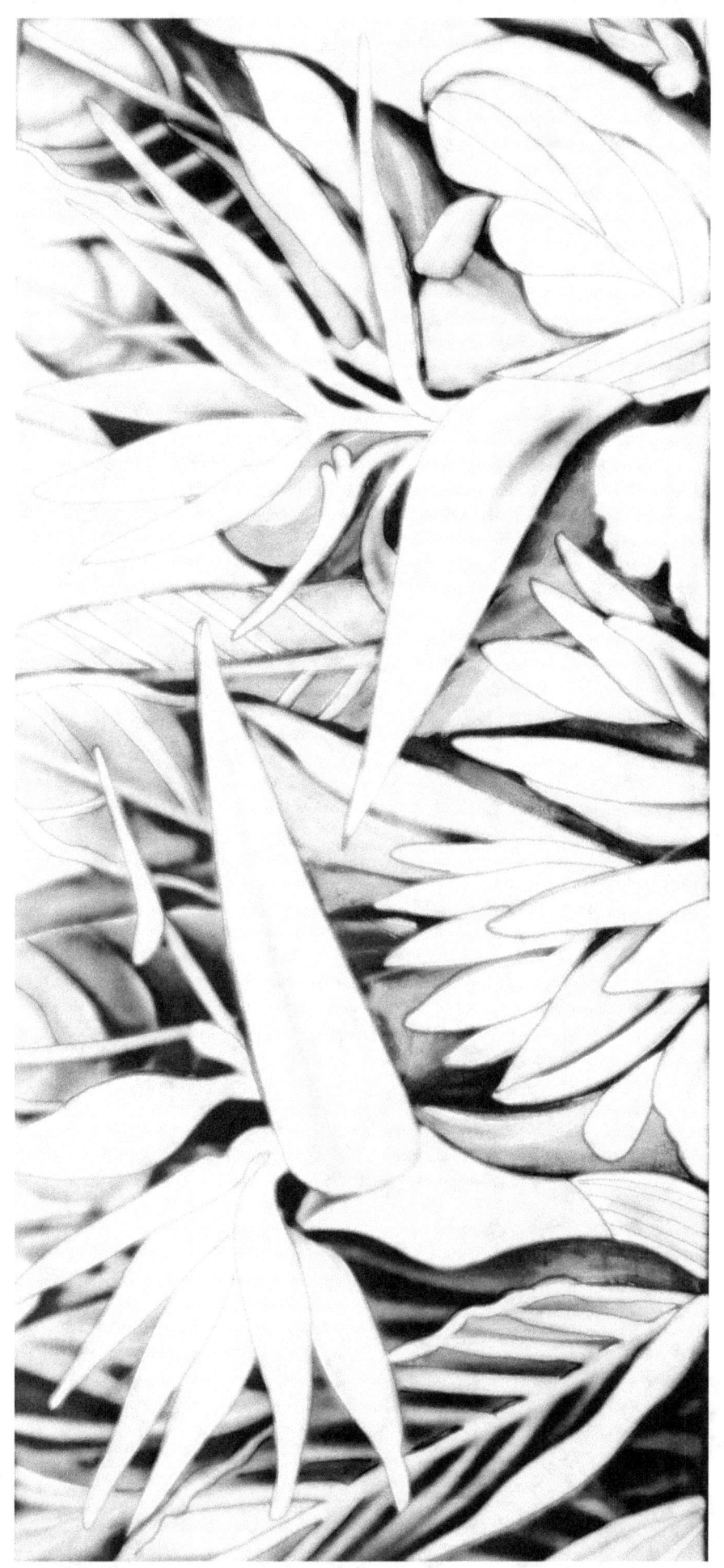

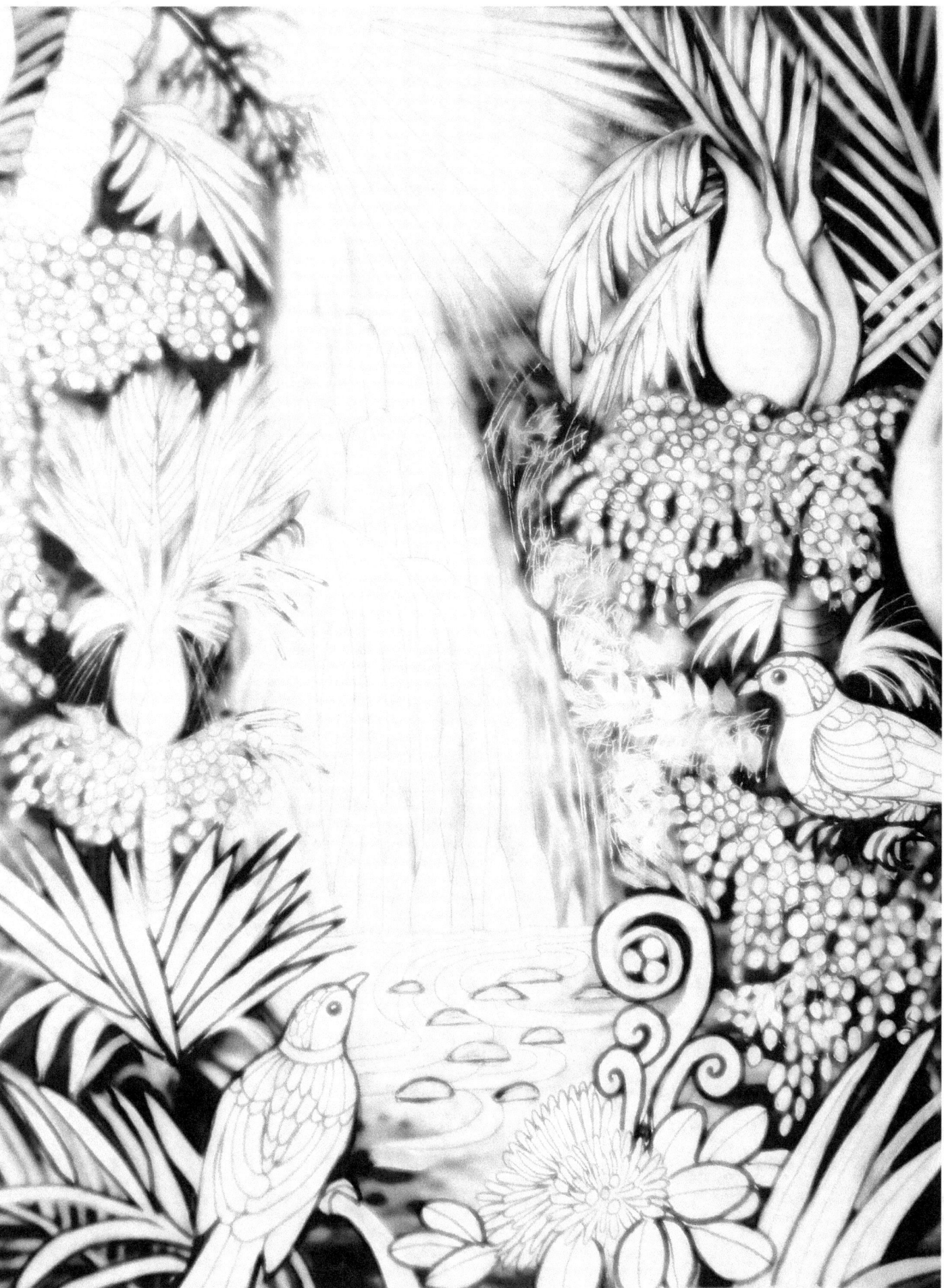

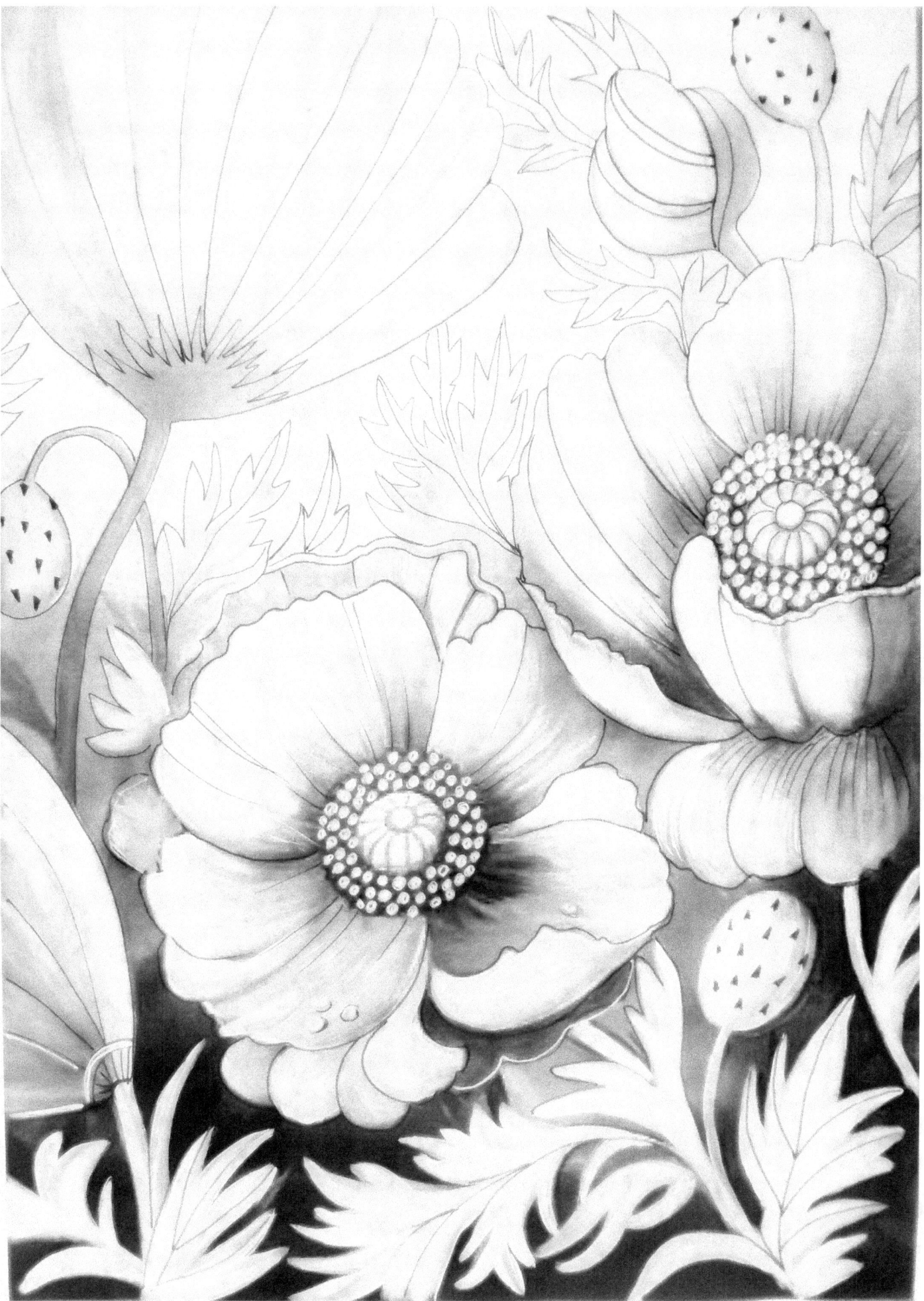

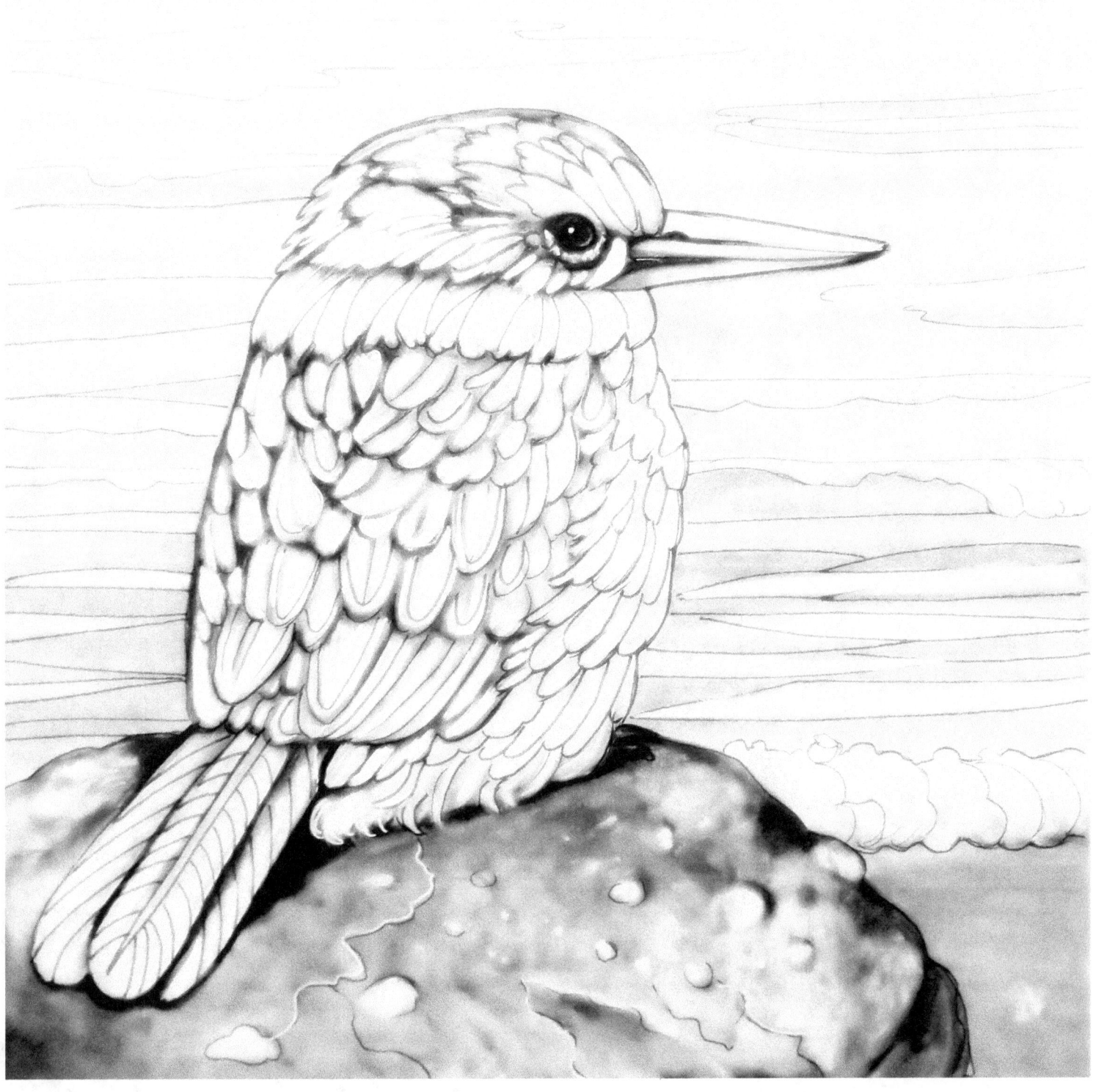

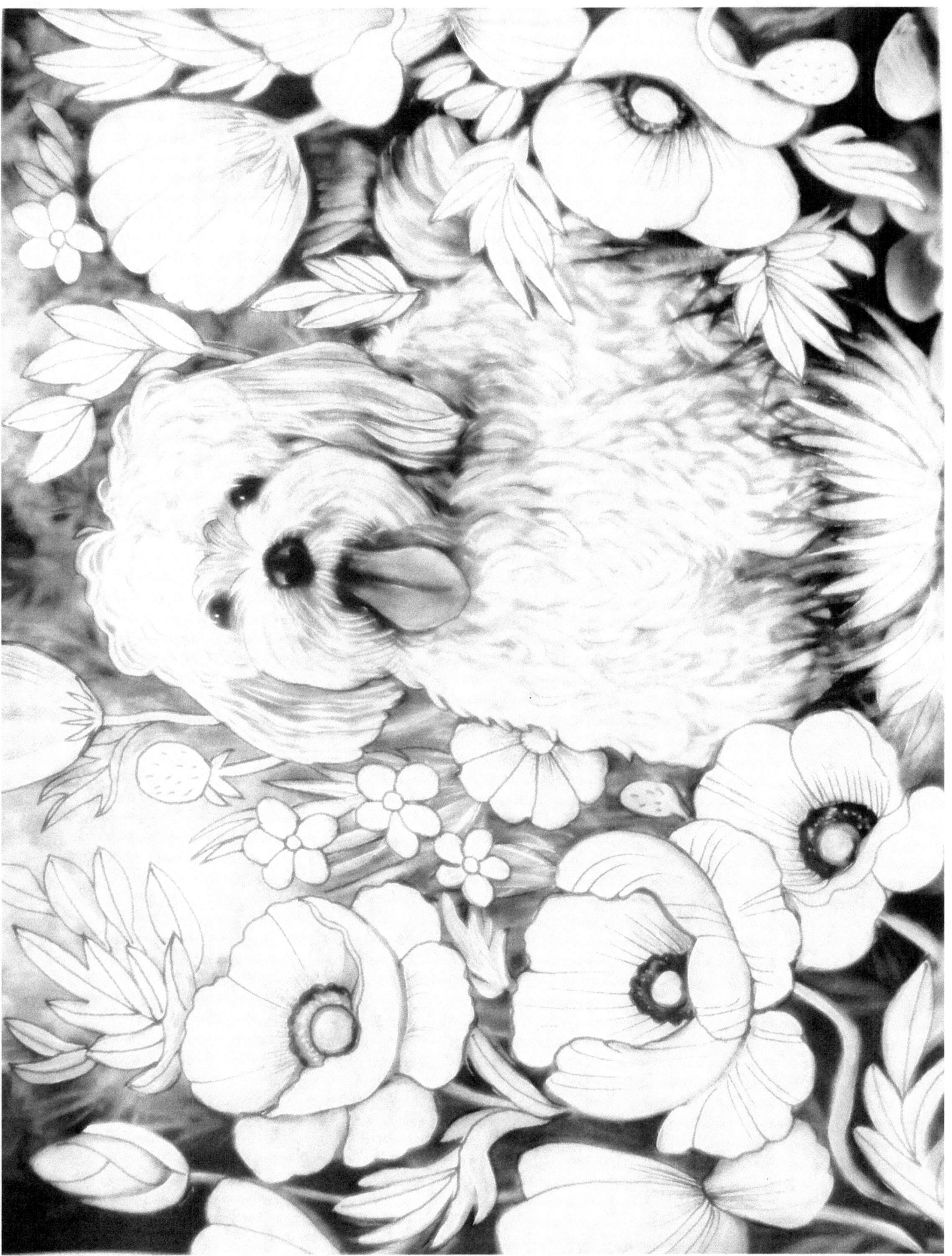

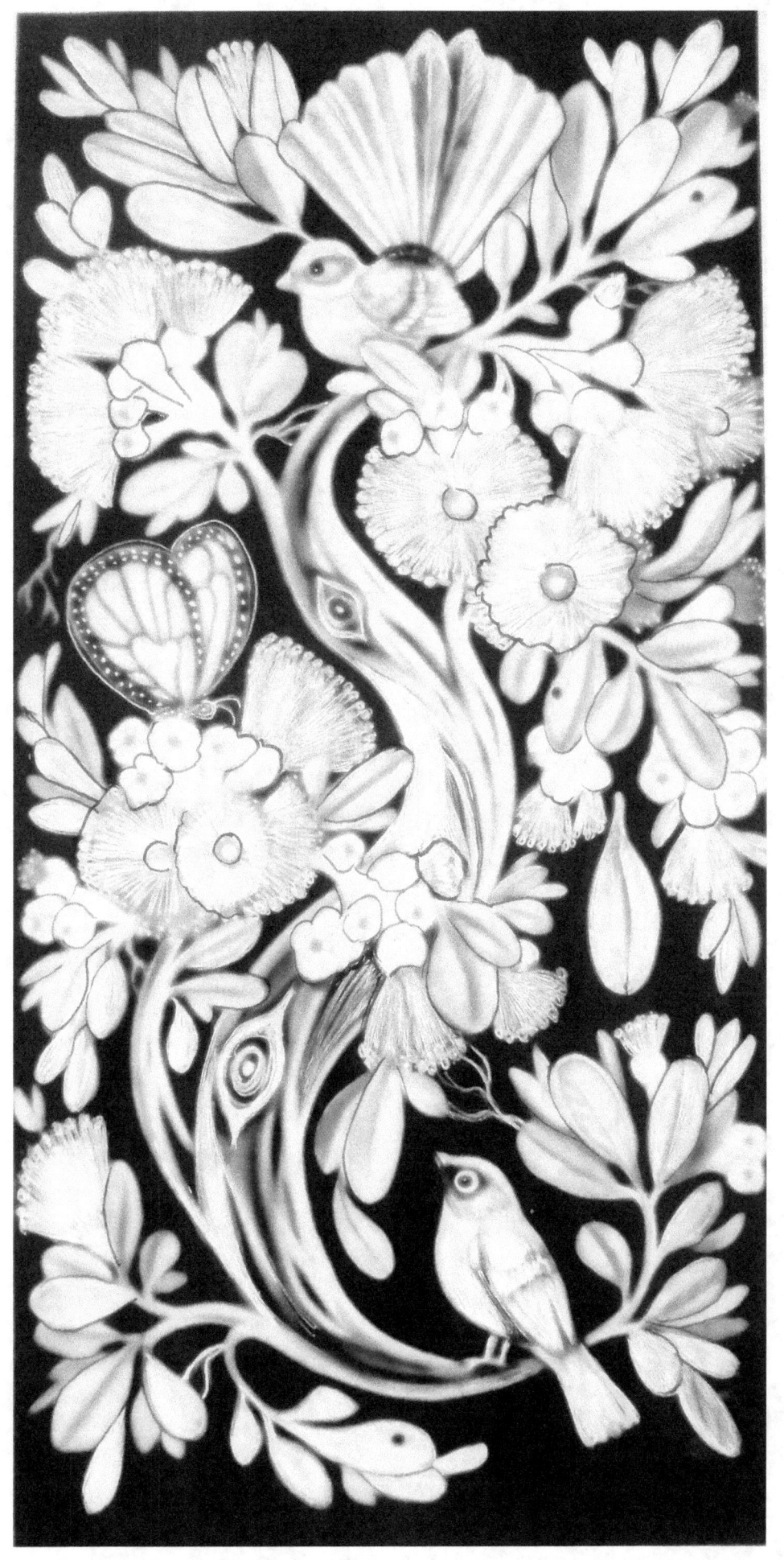

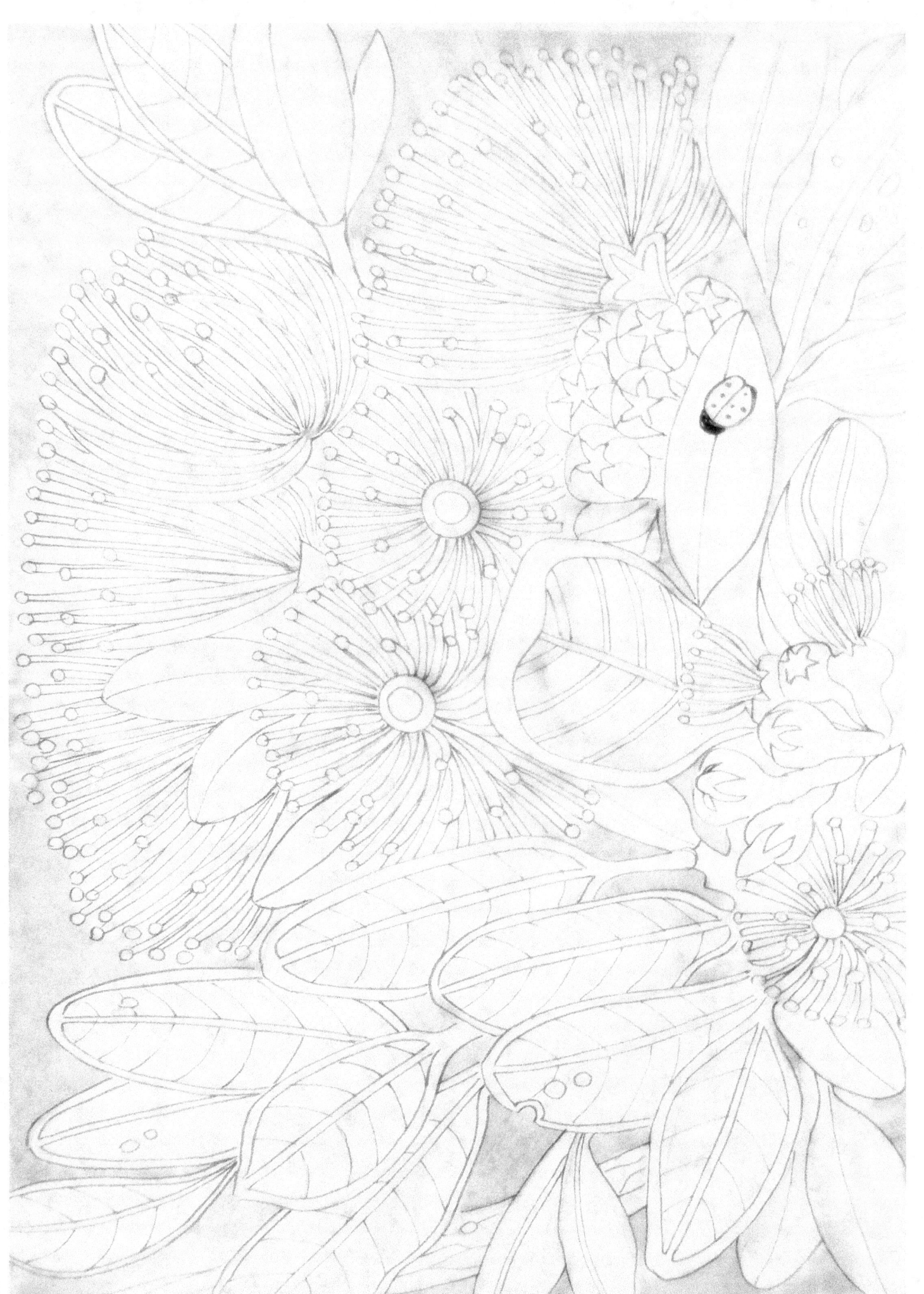

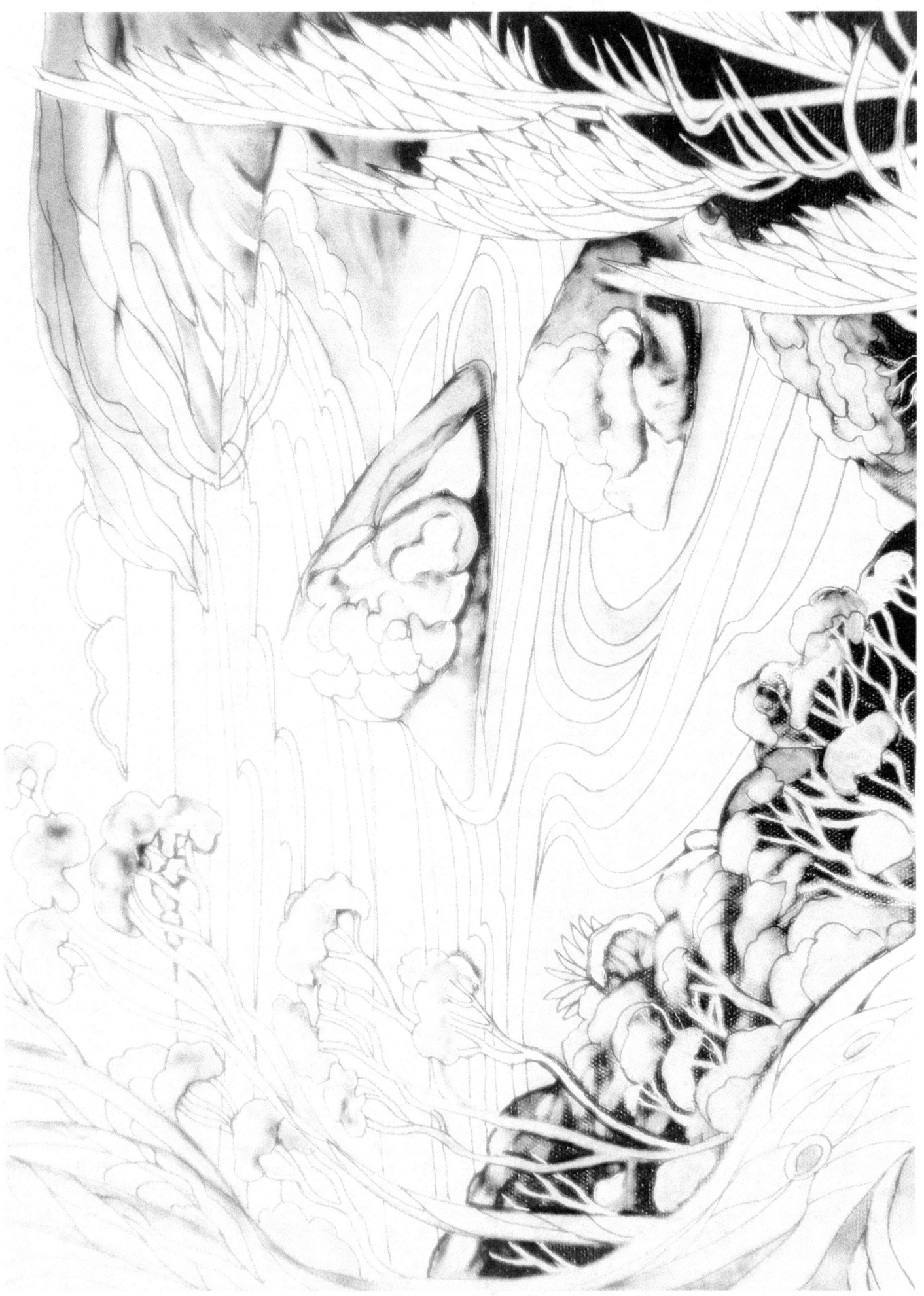

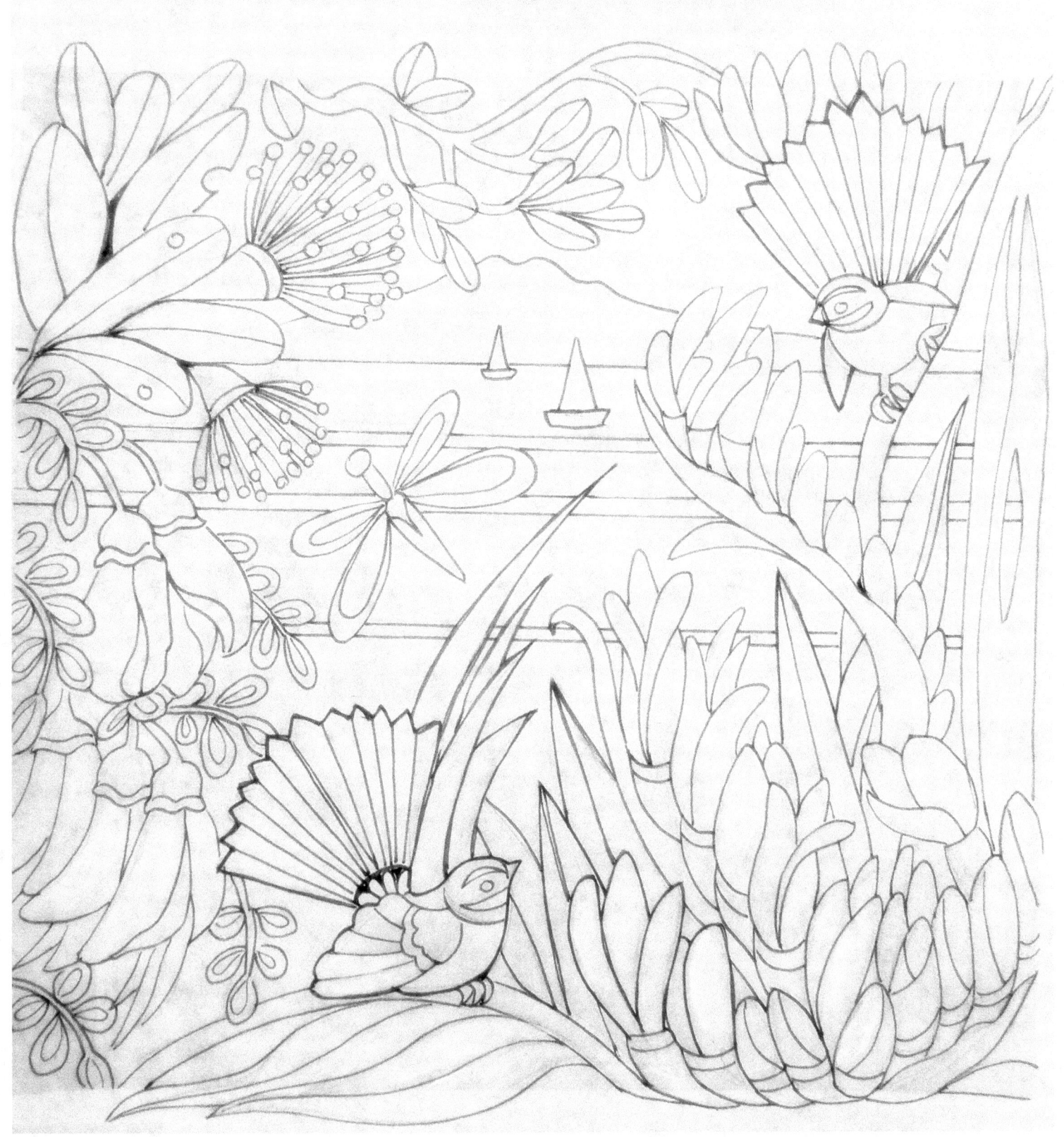

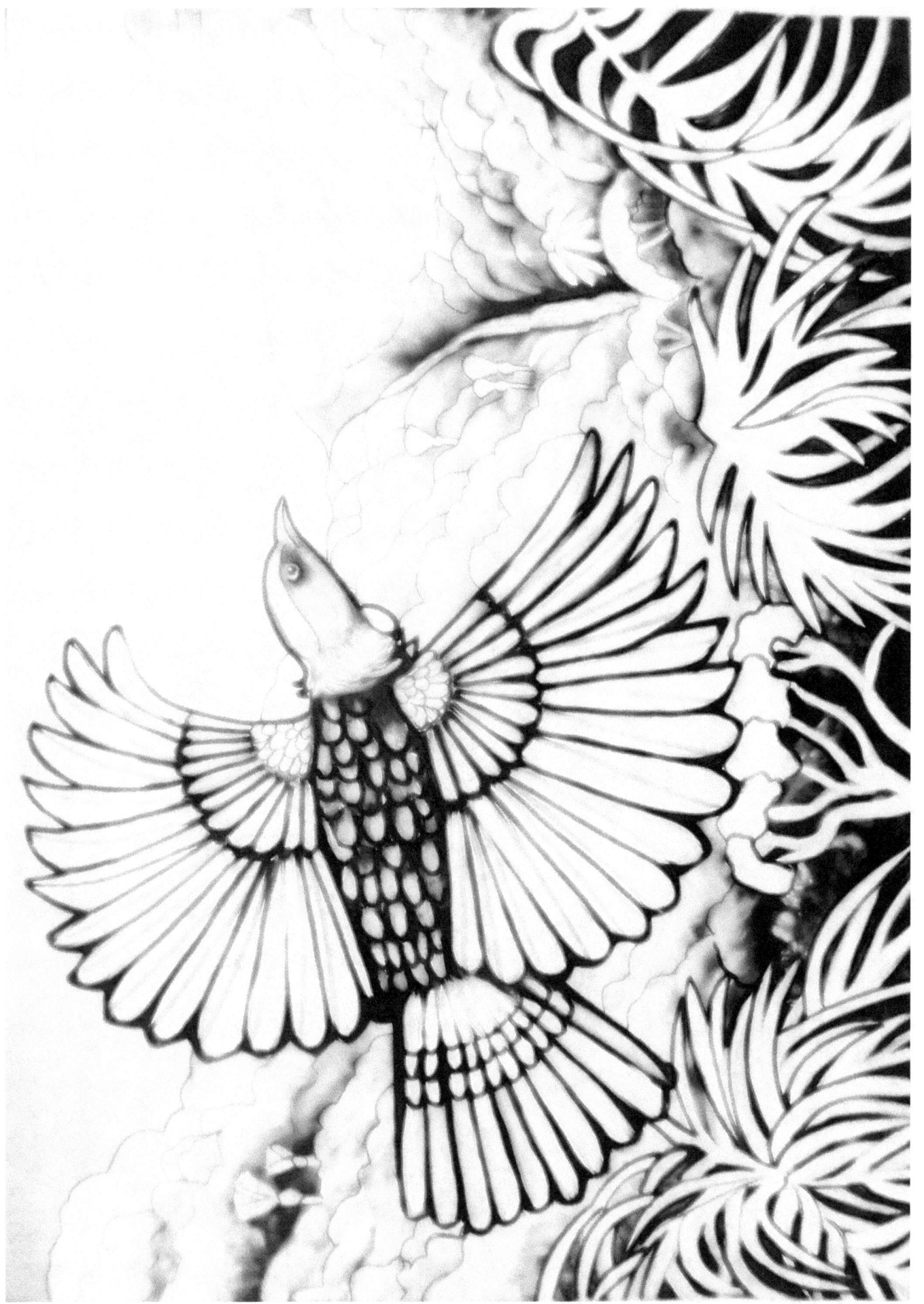

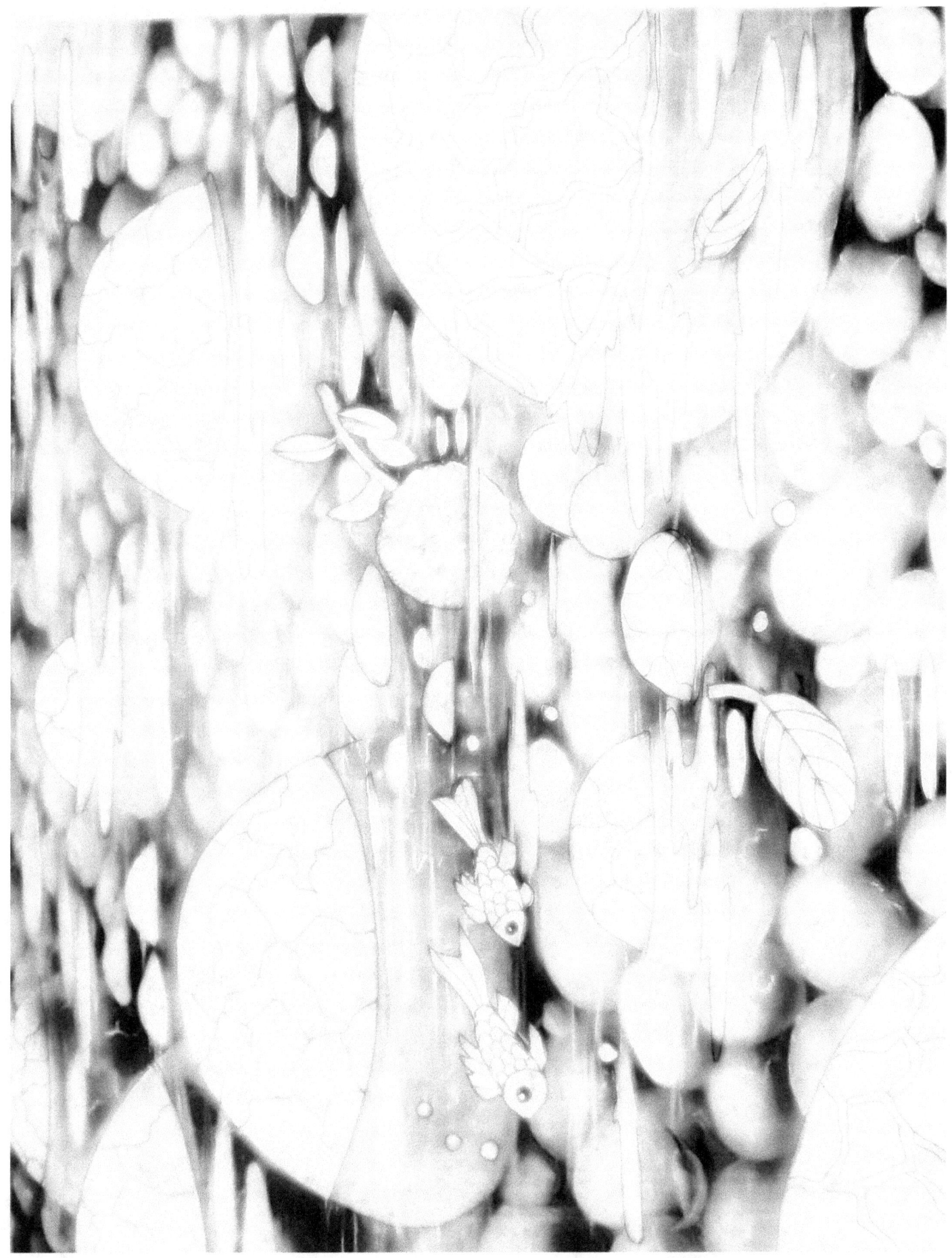

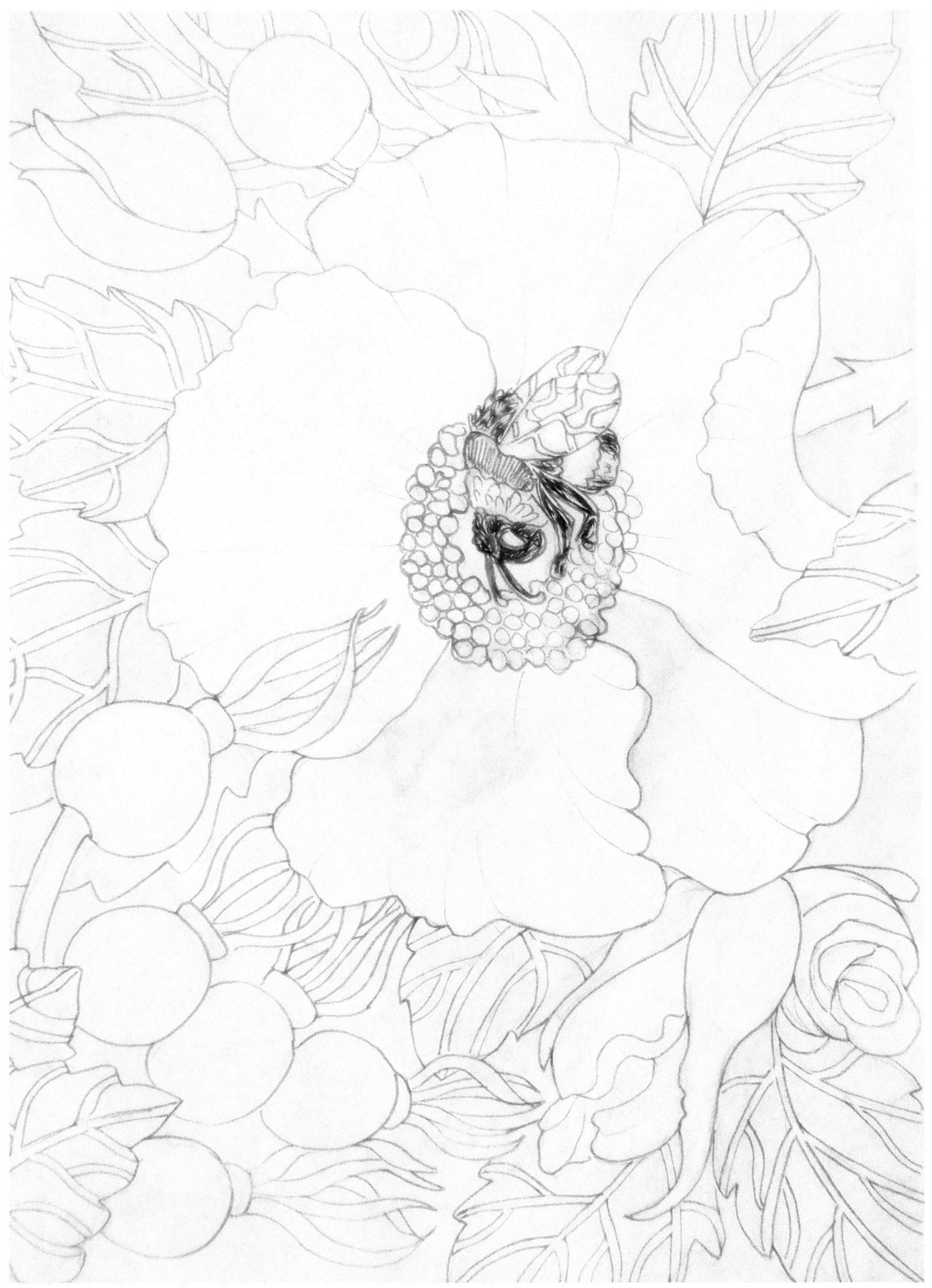

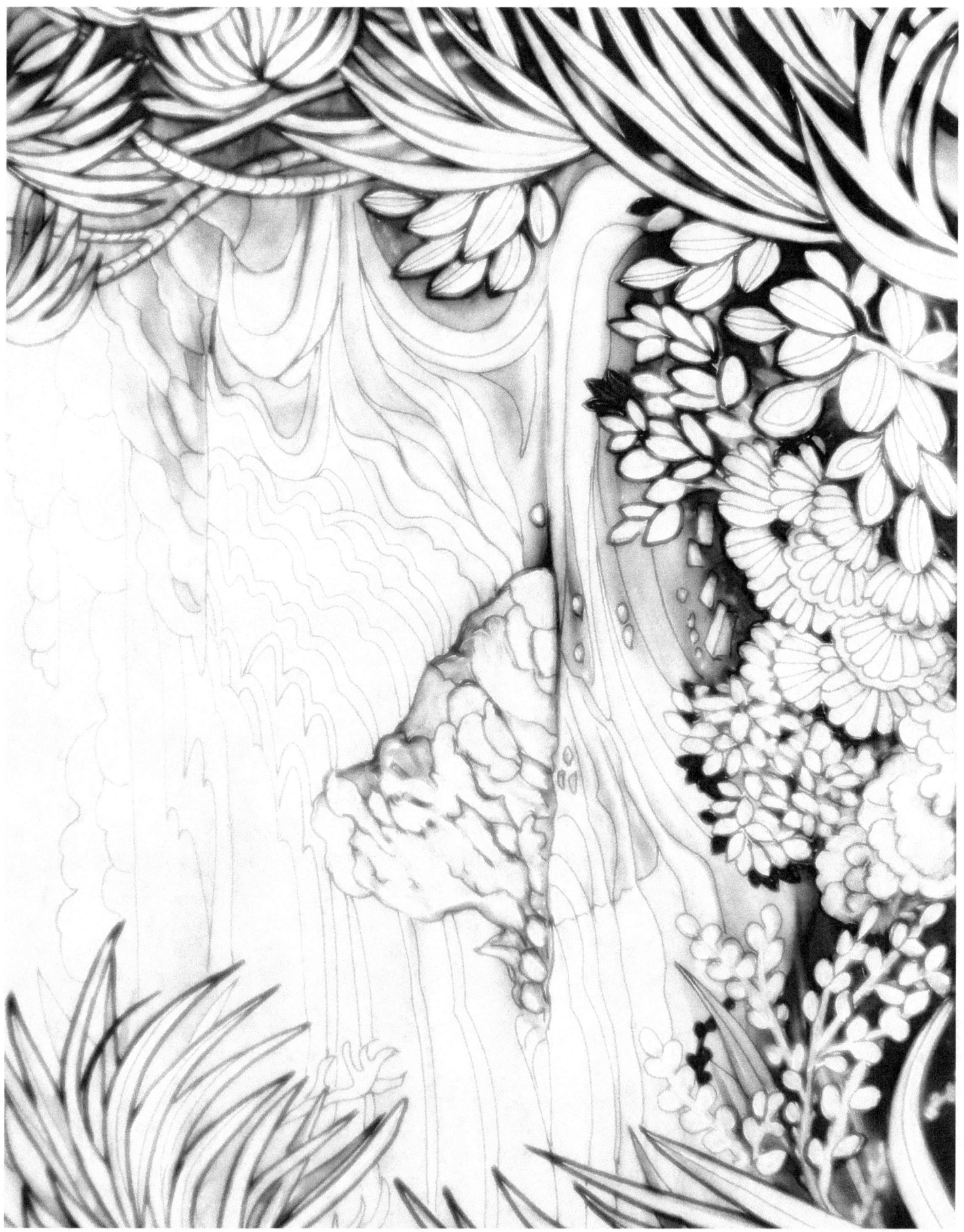

Practice here